TRANSGENDER LIFE™

TRANSGENDER ROLE MODELS AND PIONEERS

BARBRA PENNE

ROSEN PUBLISHING®

New York

Published in 2017 by The Rosen Publishing Group, Inc.
29 East 21st Street, New York, NY 10010

Library of Congress Cataloging-in-Publication Data

Names: Penne, Barbra.
Title: Transgender role models and pioneers / Barbra Penne.
Description: New York : Rosen Publishing, 2017. | Series: Transgender life | Includes index.
Identifiers: ISBN 9781508171850 (library bound) | ISBN 9781508171836 (pbk.) | ISBN 9781508171843 (6 pack)
Subjects: LCSH: Transgender people—Identity—Juvenile literature. | Transgenderism—Juvenile literature.| Role models—Juvenile literature.
Classification: LCC HQ77.9 P46 2017| DDC 306.76'8—dc23

Manufactured in China

Some of the images in this book illustrate individuals who are models. The depictions do not imply actual situations or events.

CONTENTS

INTRODUCTION

In October 2015, the *New York Times Magazine* published the article "The Year We Obsessed Over Identity." Two months later, Dictionary.com declared "identity" the word of the year. Several well-known media outlets—including CNN and *Time* magazine—followed suit. Throughout 2015, popular news stories raised awareness of issues surrounding gender, racial, and sexual identity. One of the year's biggest news stories was American athlete and reality television star Caitlyn Jenner coming out as transgender.

The term "transgender" refers to people whose gender identity is different than the one they were assigned at birth. When babies are born, they are usually assigned a gender—male or female. This is generally based on their primary sexual characteristics (such as genitalia or internal sex organs). However, gender identity is more complex than a person's anatomy. In many cases, a person's inner sense of gender matches the gender they were assigned at birth. Such people are called cisgender. However, others do not identify as the gender they were assigned at birth; they are transgender.

While many transgender individuals identify as male or female, the trans community also includes many people who don't identify with either of those two options. Those who are genderqueer or gender nonconforming may express characteristics associated with both the male and female genders through their behavior or personal style. Gender fluid individuals may change their gender identity and expression multiple times. The transgender community is diverse, as are the countless role models it has produced. While transgender figures have been in the spotlight a lot in recent years, their history stretches back much earlier than 2015.

In the late 1940s, an American army clerk from New York came across an article about a Danish doctor named Christian Hamburger, who was doing experiments with hormone therapy on animals. Hormone therapy is a treatment in which an individual receives injections of hormones that produce secondary sex characteristics. Having always felt disconnected from the male gender she was assigned as a child, Christine Jorgensen (Christine is the name she chose as part of her transition from male to female) went to Copenhagen, Denmark, in 1950 to begin receiving hormone therapy from Hamburger. After further medical procedures to affirm her female gender expression, Jorgensen returned to the United States. She quickly became a celebrity, giving interviews, working in theater and film, and launching a successful show in which she sang and did impressions. She was a pioneer and received admiration and praise from the public.

While Jorgensen found acceptance as a public icon, not every member of the transgender community does. Discrimination against transgender individuals, rejection by friends and family, and the high costs associated with certain parts of a gender transition are unfortunately common difficulties faced by the trans community.

When Christine Jorgensen transitioned from male to female in the early 1950s, she became an instant celebrity. In this August 1954 photograph, Jorgensen poses aboard the SS *United States*.

Celebrities are uniquely positioned to change public perception and raise awareness of these issues. Some members of the transgender community have become famous for their work as advocates; others were already celebrities when they transitioned gender. In either case, the work that transgender role models do to influence society and create greater awareness and acceptance is crucial. Transgender youth look to such figures to know that they, too, can live fulfilling, successful lives. Cisgender youth also learn from positive representations of the transgender community in media. By highlighting these role models, we can create a safer, more accepting society for all.

CHAPTER 1

TRANS ATHLETES

In the past, the world of sports was a limited space. Many people associate sports with masculinity, so men in the LGBTQ community and women often have been discouraged or rejected from playing sports. That changed in 1972, when the United States passed Title IX of the Education Amendments, which forbid gender discrimination in public school sports.

While the immediate impact of Title IX was the greater inclusion of women in sports in public schools and colleges, it also provides legal support for the inclusion of transgender athletes in sports. Many trailblazers have redefined how society envisions athletes to include those who identify as transgender.

RENÉE RICHARDS: TENNIS TRAILBLAZER

Renée Richards was born in 1934 in New York City. In high school, Richards excelled at several sports, including football, baseball, swimming, and tennis. In fact, she was so successful at baseball that she received an invitation to play for the New York Yankees. However, Richards declined the invite and instead decided to attend college at Yale University. At Yale, she continued to play tennis and became captain of the men's tennis team.

Despite her success at sports, Richards chose to attend medical school after graduating from Yale. She became one of the top pediatric ophthalmologists in the country, and she even enlisted in the Navy to further her medical training. However, tennis remained a great passion for her. By the early 1970s, Richards was a top-ranked professional tennis player nationally. Before transitioning from male to female, Richards was married to a woman, with whom she had a son.

SUCCESSFUL BUT UNHAPPY

To many people in her life, Richards seemed content. She was successful and athletic—she had hobbies and a family life. Richards later recalled how difficult it was for her doctors to accept her as transgender. In a May 2015 interview with *GQ*, Richards recalls, "I was not what people thought of when they thought of someone wanting to have this surgery. There was nothing 'wrong' with me." She had trouble finding doctors who were willing to help her transition from male to female. She explains:

[People] couldn't fathom how someone who had been so supremely successful in everything—in medicine, in sports, in life, as a heterosexual man, as a husband, as a father—they couldn't understand that. They couldn't understand how I could still have this overwhelming compulsion to be what I really should have been a long time ago—to have been allowed to become a woman.

Renée Richards speaks to reporters in Newport Beach, California, on August 17, 1976. At the time, the United States Tennis Association was attempting to bar Richards from playing as a woman in the US Open.

In the 1970s, many people assumed that only troubled or outwardly "feminine" men should undergo a gender transition from male to female. Friends and family couldn't understand the inner unhappiness Richards felt.

Richards was finally able to have gender-affirmation surgery in August 1975. After her surgery, she began openly expressing her female gender identity and chose the name Renée, which means "reborn" in French.

FIGHTING FOR HER RIGHT TO PLAY

After transitioning, Richards moved to California to start a new life for herself. She was popular at a local women's tennis club and won her first women's tournament. Soon after, a local reporter outed Richards as transgender. A debate followed over whether transgender athletes should be allowed to play in the league corresponding to their gender identity.

In 1976, Richards applied to play in the US Open as a woman. Competitors and critics argued that Richards had an

Richards appears on the court during an August 1976 match in South Orange, New Jersey. Richards was the first member of the transgender community to be accepted in a professional sports competition.

unfair advantage because of her physical build. In an August 1976 article, the *New York Times* posed the question: "Should Dr. Richards, an admitted transsexual [a term previously used in the medical community to describe transgender patients who had undergone gender-affirmation surgery], be permitted to compete against women who have been females from birth?"

In response to Richards's application, the United States Tennis Association (USTA) required all players to take a chromosome test, which they insisted would weed out "imposters." Richards refused and sued the USTA for discrimination. At the time, she stated, "I'm not a full-time major league tennis player. I'm here to make a point. It's a human rights issue. I want to show that someone who has a different lifestyle or medical condition has a right to stand up for what they are."

In 1977, the New York Supreme Court ruled in Richards's favor, and she was allowed to play in the 1977 US Open. She lost her first match, but left a legacy thanks to her refusal to back down in the face of discrimination. She remains humble and avoids the term pioneer. In the *GQ* interview, she shares, "I was a reluctant pioneer, so I can't take that much credit for it. I was not an activist. It was a private act for my own self-betterment, for what I wanted to do. I wanted to go and play tennis, you know?" While hesitant to take credit for her brave activism, she is proud that she laid the groundwork for other transgender athletes.

CAITLYN JENNER: AN AMERICAN HERO

Born in 1949 in Mount Kisco, New York, Caitlyn Jenner was a natural athlete from a young age. Evidently, it was in her genes. Her father had competed in the US Army Olympics, and her grandfather had run in the Boston Marathon. In a 1999 interview

TRANSGENDER DISCRIMINATION IN SPORTS

One of the biggest challenges LGBTQ athletes face is finding acceptance in sports communities. The problem is particularly noticeable on school campuses, where bullying can be prevalent and educators don't always know how to combat these issues.

The NCAA Sport Science Institute's guide to student-athlete mental health issues directly addresses discrimination against LGBTQ students. Studies cited in the guide found that "despite the diversity of ethnicity, socioeconomic status, geographic background and even sexual orientation, coaches, administrators and student-athletes nonetheless often exhibit heterosexist and homophobic attitudes." In almost all sports and schools studied, team members expressed negative opinions regarding LGBTQ teammates. The NCAA also noted the prevalence of drug and alcohol use, depression, and suicidal thoughts among LGBTQ athletes.

Nonetheless, the law stands on the side of LGBTQ student athletes. As the Women's Sports Foundation's guide on the rights of transgender student-athletes notes, trans athletes are protected by Title IX and must be provided with access to locker rooms corresponding to their gender identity. Furthermore, the guide dispels the myth that transgender women have an unfair physical advantage over cisgender women in sports. Not only on school campuses do transgender athletes have rights. Since 2003, the International Olympic Committee has had a policy in place for the inclusion of transgender athletes.

with *Ability* magazine, Jenner notes, "By the time I turned two, I'd already developed a big chest, wide shoulders, and boundless energy." Later in life, Jenner would reveal that at around eight years old, she first began to experiment with female gender expression, trying on her mother's clothing in secret.

In high school, Jenner knew that she wasn't fully comfortable with her assigned gender but couldn't quite express what was wrong. In an April 2015 ABC News interview, Jenner explained her confusion about gender identity and sexual orientation. She

Olympic gold medalist and reality television sensation Caitlyn Jenner plays in the Ladies Professional Golf Association's ANA Inspiration Official Pro-Am tournament in Rancho Mirage, California, in March 2016.

shares, "I was never attracted to the guys or any of that kind of stuff, OK? Because sexuality was totally different from what my issues were."

SPORTS LEGEND

Jenner attended Graceland University on a football scholarship. A knee injury derailed her football aspirations, but ultimately brought Jenner to track and field, a sport where she excelled. Jenner continued training after college. In 1972, she became part of the US men's decathlon team at the Olympics. Her tenth-place finish inspired her to work harder, train harder, and improve her running times.

After the Olympics, Jenner married Chrystie Crownover and began intense training in San Jose, California. In 1976, she returned to the Olympics to compete in the men's decathlon. Jenner set a new world record and took home the gold medal, becoming a national hero. She scored lucrative promotional deals, becoming a spokesperson for various brands—most notably Wheaties cereal—and appearing on the cover of many magazines, including *Sports Illustrated*.

Despite her success in the public eye, Jenner was suffering in private. After six years of marriage, Jenner and her wife had a child. Soon, another child was on the way. Around this time, Chrystie became the first person to whom Jenner opened up about her gender dysphoria, but even Caitlyn wasn't certain about transitioning at the time. In 1980, Jenner and Crownover divorced. Although Crownover was supportive, both partners recognized that their marriage didn't work for them.

In 1981, Jenner married songwriter Linda Thompson. With Thompson, Jenner had two more children. However, Jenner experienced an even greater sense of gender dysphoria. After four years of marriage, Jenner revealed her gender dysphoria to Linda, and the couple went to counseling together. After six months of therapy, Thompson understood that Jenner's gender identity was not a phase, but a permanent part of who she was. The couple divorced, but Thompson respected Jenner's privacy and did not out her as a transgender woman.

BECOMING A KARDASHIAN

Following her divorce from Thompson, Jenner became depressed and distant from her four children. She began to transition from male to female, undergoing hormone therapy and minor cosmetic procedures. But when the media began reporting on Jenner's changing appearance, she became worried that she would be outed and stopped her transition. She knew it wasn't time yet.

In 1990, Jenner was set up on a date with Kris Kardashian, a divorcée with four children from her own first marriage. While Jenner was initially put off by Kardashian's interests in fashion and shopping, the two clicked, and in 1991, they got married. Once married, the couple had two children together. Kris became a driving force in Jenner's life, bringing Caitlyn lucrative business deals and coming up with creative ways to profit off Jenner's former success as an athlete.

In 2007, Kris's most innovative idea became a reality. In October of that year, *Keeping Up with the Kardashians* debuted. The reality show followed the lives of the Jenner-Kardashian family and became an immediate success. Viewership was high, and each family member found their own profitable business endeavors thanks to the fame that the show brought them. Nonetheless, the attention made Caitlyn Jenner uncomfortable.

She was often depicted as out of touch and an outsider in her own family. By 2013, Jenner's marriage was dissolving and late that year, she and Kris announced their divorce.

LIFE AS CAIT

In 2014, Jenner began her second attempt to transition from male to female. She began hormone therapy, grew her hair out, and began subtly expressing herself as a woman through nail polish, jewelry, and makeup. Paparazzi reports on her transition

Following the public announcement of her gender identity in April 2015, Jenner became an advocate for the transgender community, sharing her own story and shining a light on issues that affect the community.

made her fearful, and she considered halting her transition once again. But she knew she needed to follow through and be true to herself.

In early 2015, Jenner gathered her family and came out to them as transgender. In March, she underwent certain gender reassignment surgeries to make her appearance more feminine. Then, in April 2015, Jenner's moment came. She appeared on the television show *20/20* for an interview with Diane Sawyer in which she publicly came out as a trans woman. In July, she generated one of that year's most-talked-about moments when she appeared on the cover of *Vanity Fair* with the words, "Call me Caitlyn," printed across her photo.

Following her transition, Jenner received widespread public support from her family and other celebrities. She also began starring in her own reality show, *I Am Cait*, which she has used as a platform to highlight the struggles faced by members of the transgender community. Jenner is credited with bringing unprecedented attention to the rights of the transgender community.

A NEW GENERATION OF TRANS ATHLETES

With growing awareness of the rights of the transgender community, a new generation of trans athletes has made progress in the world of athletics. In 2010, George Washington University basketball player Kye Allums came out as a transgender man while a teammate on the school's women's basketball team. Upon coming out, Allums became the first openly trans basketball player to play on an NCAA Division I team. Allums's teammates and school showed support for him and, along with

In 2010, basketball player Kye Allums made history by becoming the first openly transgender athlete on an NCAA Division I team. Here, Allums is photographed ahead of a January 2011 game in Washington, D.C.

the NCAA, defended his right to play on the women's team until he chose to begin hormone therapy. Allums delayed his medical transition until he was no longer playing for GWU. Since his time on the court, Allums has become a motivational speaker, sharing his story and defending the rights of transgender athletes to participate in sports. In July 2015, he was inducted into the National Gay and Lesbian Sports Hall of Fame.

Bodybuilder and men's health vlogger Aydian Dowling has also challenged stereotypes about the transgender community and its participation in athletics. In 2015, Dowling received unprecedented support in a competition to appear on the cover of *Men's Health* magazine. Doing so would have made him the first transgender man to appear on the magazine's cover. While he ultimately lost the contest, Dowling received seventy-two thousand votes. He appeared on a collector's edition cover with all other participants, where he was identified as a "pioneer." Dowling subsequently appeared on the cover of *Gay Times* magazine and has remained a prominent activist and vlogger, promoting the inclusion of transgender men and women in the world of athletics.

CHAPTER 2

TRANS PEOPLE IN TELEVISION AND FILM

The world of entertainment has an allure for people from all walks of life. It provides an outlet for actors and directors to express their worldview, comment on life as it exists, and create alternate realities. Entertainers on screen deliver messages that help shape public opinion and trends. In fact, the entertainment industry has helped foster the growing awareness and acceptance of the transgender community in recent years.

THE WACHOWSKIS: CREATING ALTERNATE WORLDS

Throughout the 1990s, a duo of filmmaking siblings from Chicago, Illinois, struggled to find their place in Hollywood. Coming from a background in video games and comic books, Lana and Lilly Wachowski had long been fascinated with crafting alternate realities. As children, they were avid players of Dungeons & Dragons and fans of sci-fi films, especially *2001: A Space Odyssey*.

The siblings' first stint as screenwriters, the 1994 action thriller *Assassins*, was unsuccessful. However, their debut as directors with the 1996 crime thriller *Bound* was well received by critics. It also gave the duo, who both still publicly identified as heterosexual men, an opportunity to depict a lesbian relationship as a central plot element to great acclaim from the LGBTQ community.

ENTERING THE MATRIX

In 1999, the Wachowskis released the result of years of work, *The Matrix*. The movie is set in a dystopian future where machines use human beings for their energy, all the while keeping the humans in coma-like states hooked up to a simulated reality similar to our real world. A small group of humans—aware of the humans' enslavement by machines—fight to free humanity. The Wachowskis were sure that the film would be a success— and they were right. It earned over $30 million in its opening weekend. But with its success came much unwanted attention for Lana and Lilly. They had always valued their privacy, and the popularity of *The Matrix* threatened that.

The siblings moved to Australia to shoot two sequels, and during this period, Lana acknowledged having experienced intense gender dysphoria. In a September 2012 profile by *The New Yorker*, Lana shares, "When I began to admit [that I was transgender] to myself, I knew I would eventually have to tell my parents and my brother and my sisters. This fact would inject such terror into me that I would not sleep for days." Sensing something was wrong, her family flew to Australia. When they arrived, Lana came out to them, and they embraced her with love and acceptance. She soon began to transition from male to female, choosing to stay out of the public's eye as she always had.

Director, screenwriter, and producer Lana Wachowski has blazed a trail for transgender women in Hollywood. Here, Wachoswki smiles at the premiere of her 2015 film *Jupiter Ascending*.

GIVING UP THEIR PRIVACY

As Lana transitioned, tabloids and blogs widely reported on the changes in her appearance, but Lana refused to address the rumors. She divorced her first wife and continued to work on film projects with Lilly, who had not yet come out as transgender. In the years to come, the Wachowskis worked in various capacities on the films *V for Vendetta* (2006), *Speed Racer* (2008), and *Cloud Atlas* (2012). In 2009, Lana married her second wife.

Lana increasingly felt the need to share her story and publicly speak about her gender identity. The story of a transgender teen who was murdered in a hate crime inspired Lana to use her platform as a director, screenwriter, and film producer to promote transgender rights. Without any specific statement, Lana participated in a promotional video for *Cloud Atlas*, allowing the public to see her for the first time since her transition from male to female. In the following years, she shared her story, most notably while receiving the Human Rights Campaign (HRC) Visibility Award in 2012.

In March 2016, Lilly Wachowski also came out as a transgender woman. After a journalist confronted her at her home about her gender identity, Lilly chose to come out on her own terms, releasing a statement and self-portrait to the *Windy City Times*, a well-respected LGBT newspaper. Nobody should ever be forced out of the closet.

While the Wachowskis have revolutionized science fiction with their innovative screenplays and iconic special effects, their roles as transgender women in filmmaking have allowed them to blaze a different kind of trail for generations of screenwriters, directors, and producers to come.

Lilly Wachowski accepts the award for Outstanding Drama Series at the 27th Annual GLAAD Media Awards in Los Angeles, California, on April 2, 2016.

CHAZ BONO: BECOMING HIMSELF

As the child of the popular entertaining duo Sonny and Cher, Chaz Bono was in the spotlight from a young age. Born in 1969 in Los Angeles, California, Chaz spent his childhood as a regular guest on his parents' *The Sonny & Cher Comedy Hour*, a popular variety show. As a teenager, Chaz identified as a lesbian, coming out to his parents when he was eighteen years old but never coming out to the public.

Bono's first exposure to the spotlight for his own accomplishments came in the early 1990s through minor success with a band, Ceremony. Ceremony never quite hit it big, and Bono soon found a different kind of public calling. In 1995 — after having been outed by several tabloid magazines — Bono appeared on the cover of *Advocate*, a popular LGBTQ-themed magazine, identifying as a lesbian woman. He became a writer for *Advocate*, a spokesperson for the HRC, and the entertainment media director for the LGBTQ-rights organization GLAAD. He also penned two books in which he opened up about his own experience of coming out.

Despite public support, Bono struggled privately. The untimely losses of both his father and a romantic partner marked a dark period in Bono's life. In his 2011 autobiography, *Transition*, Bono says his life was overtaken by binge eating, depression, and prescription painkiller abuse. However, with the help of longtime girlfriend Jennifer Elia, Bono began to steer his life in the right direction.

In 2006, Bono appeared on the popular television show *Celebrity Fit Club* and began to shed his excess weight. In 2008, he took another important step for his physical and mental health. Bono began to transition from female to male. In February 2016, Bono opened up about his struggle to lose weight and get fit on *Oprah: Where Are They Now?* He shared, "I would have never been able to do it before [transitioning]… I was too disconnected from my body, and the dysphoria that I had with my body was too much to be able to have cared enough to do anything like that."

Bono has been very public about his transition, documenting it thoroughly in a 2011 documentary titled *Becoming Chaz* as well as in his autobiography, *Transition*. In 2011, he became the first transgender person to appear on a major network television show for something unrelated to his gender identity when he competed on *Dancing with the Stars*. While he did not win the competition on the show, Bono has used the publicity it brought him to promote awareness of transgender rights and the importance of physical and mental health.

LAVERNE COX: A VOICE FOR THE VOICELESS

Laverne Cox was born and grew up in Mobile, Alabama, with her mother, Gloria, and her twin brother, Reginald (who is a performer under the stage name M Lamar). Both Laverne and her brother were assigned male at birth.

In a May 2014 interview for *Time*, Cox described herself as a creative child with a love of dancing. However, she also recalls, "I was very feminine and I was really bullied, majorly bullied."

Cox poses outside the premiere of her 2016 film *FREE CeCe!*, a documentary about CeCe McDonald, an African American transgender prisoner who faced discrimination in the criminal justice system.

Laverne was taunted and called names because of her femininity. Today, she routinely shares the moment in third grade when her teacher called her mother to remark, "Your son is going to end up in New Orleans wearing a dress." Cox came to think that being transgender was shameful.

Throughout her teenage years, Laverne went to therapy and struggled with gender dysphoria privately. She even attempted suicide once but thankfully survived. She became an overachiever, focusing on dance and academics to prove her own worth.

EXPERIMENTING WITH GENDER EXPRESSION

For high school, Laverne and her brother went to a special arts school in Birmingham, Alabama. There, she developed her interest in ballet. Living on campus, an hour away from home, she also first experimented with her gender expression. In a July 2014 interview with *Advocate*, she observes, "I definitely did not identify as male, but I didn't identify as a woman yet either, not until later… I was very androgynous in high school, and continued in college."

Cox attended Marymount Manhattan College in New York City, where she developed her passion for acting and changed majors from dance to theater. Cox also found greater acceptance outside school. New York City nightlife gave her the freedom to express herself as androgynous without judgment from others. After college, Cox began the process of transitioning from male to female. While it was challenging for her at first, Laverne's mother ultimately became one of her biggest supporters.

RISING TO FAME

After transitioning, Cox scored a number of minor television and film roles. Her most notable early appearances were on the reality

TRANS PEOPLE ON TELEVISION AND IN FILM: A TIMELINE

Before the 2000s, there were few positive representations of transgender characters in entertainment, although two notable examples stand out. In 1975, a two-part episode of the medical drama *Medical Center* featured actor Robert Reed as a transgender doctor who undergoes gender-reassignment surgery. Reed won two Emmy Awards for his guest appearance. In 1977, popular sitcom *The Jeffersons* aired the episode "Once a Friend," in which an old Navy buddy of main character George Jefferson comes back to town, only to reveal that she has transitioned from male to female.

In the 1980s and '90s, transgender characters were most often used as punch lines or depicted as victims of hate crimes. Some exceptions did provide meaningful representations of trans characters. The 1997 Belgian film *Ma vie en rose* depicts a transgender girl whose family insists on treating her as a boy. *Boys Don't Cry* (1999) depicted the story of Brandon Teena, a transgender man targeted, raped, and murdered for his gender identity.

Nevertheless, in 2012, GLAAD reported that, of 102 instances of transgender characters appearing on television from 2002 to 2012, 54 percent negatively portrayed transgender characters as victims, murderers, or prostitutes. Laverne Cox's role on *Orange Is the New Black* (2013) has been monumental in changing the dialogue.

(continued on the next page)

(continued from the previous page)

Popular shows such as *Transparent* (2014) and *Sense8* (2015), which, respectively, star transgender actors Trace Lysette and Jamie Clayton, have become widely successful. Both shows feature positive representations of transgender characters whose character development is not limited to issues surrounding gender identity.

competition *I Want to Work for Diddy* (2008), on which contestants auditioned for a position as Sean "Diddy" Combs's assistant, and *TRANSform Me* (2010), Cox's own show on which she and two other trans women gave cisgender women makeovers. Cox was the first black transgender woman to produce and star in her own show.

In 2013, Cox finally hit it big. Her role as transgender inmate Sophia Burset on the Netflix series *Orange Is the New Black* made her a household name. The series depicts the lives of a diverse group of women living together in a federal prison. As Sophia, Cox was able to shed light on the unique struggles and discrimination faced by transgender inmates. In one episode, prison budget cuts threaten Sophia's ability to get her hormone therapy pills. Another episode highlights the prison guards' inability to protect her from violence by other inmates. Critically acclaimed for her role, Cox became one of the most influential and recognizable transgender celebrities in the world. She has received numerous awards and nominations for her work on the show.

Cox has used the platform the show has given her to shine a light on the discrimination against the transgender community and especially transgender people of color. She toured universities throughout North America with her speech "Ain't I a Woman? My Journey to Womanhood," which highlights the inequalities faced by African American transgender women. She also visited mainstream television talk shows, bringing these topics to America's living rooms. In 2014, Cox received the GLAAD Stephen F. Kolzak Award for highlighting discrimination against the LGBTQ community in Hollywood.

In 2015, Cox appeared nude in *Allure* magazine to promote positive body image for transgender women, especially those who are black. In the accompanying write-up, Cox says, "Seeing a black transgender woman embracing and loving everything about herself might be inspiring to some other folks. There's beauty in the things we think are imperfect."

CHAPTER 3

TRANS MUSICIANS

Music is an escape for everybody. Through headphones, car speakers, or the booming sound system at a live concert, we leave our reality, stress, and responsibilities behind and find happiness and freedom through melodies and lyrics. Just as listeners find an escape through music, musicians, too, have found release through their work. And many transgender musicians have found acceptance in the music community and used their artistry to inspire others.

WENDY CARLOS: PIONEER OF ELECTRONIC MUSIC

Wendy Carlos, the so-called godmother of electronic music, was a transgender pioneer in the music industry. Carlos was born in 1939 in Rhode Island to a musical family. Her mother played the piano, and she had uncles who played the trombone, the trumpet, and the drums.

Wendy Carlos smiles amid keyboards and synthesizers. Carlos is celebrated as a pioneer of electronic music and one of the first openly transgender musicians.

Starting at age nine, Wendy focused on playing piano but also showed an inclination for computers and technology. In a July 1985 interview with *People*, she shares, "Inside I had the feeling that I was a little girl. I preferred long hair and girl's clothes and didn't understand my parents treating me like a boy. I kept my feelings to myself." She channeled her creativity into her music.

Carlos attended Brown University, where she studied music and physics. In college, Carlos discovered electronic music. She told *People*, "I didn't decide. It chased me. I loved all the musical, mechanical, and dramatic things about the field."

After graduating from Brown, Carlos went on to a master's program at the Columbia-Princeton Electronic Music Center at Columbia University, in New York City. During this time, Carlos became friendly with Robert Moog, who was developing the Moog synthesizer, an important instrument in electronic music. In 1967, Columbia paid Carlos to recreate Johann Sebastian Bach's classical music on the synthesizer. The resulting album, *Switched-On Bach*, was released in October 1968 to unexpected success. It won three Grammy Awards and popularized the synthesizer as an instrument.

Despite her newfound success, Carlos was unhappy. She was receiving counseling from Dr. Harry Benjamin, a well-known expert in gender transitions, and began her own gender transition from male to female in 1968. As hormone-replacement therapy caused Carlos's appearance to change, those close to her convinced her that it would be detrimental to her career to reveal her gender identity. She became withdrawn and appeared in public only disguised as a man. She continued to release music—a total of eight albums—under her former name, Walter Carlos. In 1972, she used the money she earned from *Switched-On Bach* to pay for gender-reassignment surgery. But discouraged by others from coming out publicly as transgender, Carlos remained unhappy and avoided the spotlight.

In 1979, Carlos finally came out as transgender in an interview with *Playboy* magazine. In 1985, she told *People*, "The public turned out to be amazingly tolerant or, if you wish, indifferent. There had never been any need of this charade to have taken place. It had proven a monstrous waste of years of my life." Already a successful composer, Carlos continued to produce groundbreaking music after publicly coming out as a transgender woman. Among her many accomplishments are the film scores for *A Clockwork Orange* (1971), *The Shining* (1980), and *Disney's Tron* (1982).

Her first studio album after coming out, 1984's *Digital Moonscapes*, was a monumental achievement. For it, Carlos created a "digitally synthesized orchestra." She composed the score and created over five hundred digital "voices," building a complex web of lyrical sounds. Two more albums released in the late 1980s built on her work with *Digital Moonscapes*, creating new scales and working with advanced digital synthesizers. Although she continued to remaster her older work, Carlos has remained mostly out of the spotlight since the 1990s. However, her legacy is felt in the popularity of dance and electronic music today.

TRANSGENDER ARTISTS IN PUNK AND OTHER ALTERNATIVE GENRES

Rock music—and punk rock, in particular—has always had a special place for anti-Establishment feelings. Rock and its subgenres have often carved out a space for those who don't fit into mainstream society, so it's no shocker that transgender musicians and music fans have found acceptance in the rock scene. One notable example stands out: Laura Jane Grace, lead signer of the punk rock band Against Me!

Grace was born in 1980 and assigned male at birth. In 1997, she formed Against Me! as a solo act before later expanding the band to a quartet. From 1997 to 2010, the band released five albums and developed a dedicated following of fans. However, in 2010, Grace became distant from her bandmates, cancelling tour dates and often checking into hotels alone. The band separated from its record label and began to create music

Laura Jane Grace sings during a performance at the 2016 Governors Ball music festival in New York City. Her band Against Me!'s 2014 album *Transgender Dysphoria Blues* discussed gender dysphoria.

independently. In May 2012, Grace came out as a transgender woman and explained that many of the band's issues in 2010 were a result of her gender dysphoria. That same year, she began publicly transitioning from male to female.

Against Me! has continued to find success in the punk rock scene. After North Carolina passed a transphobic "bathroom bill" in 2016, Grace and her band chose not to cancel a local concert (as many other musicians had done, in protest). Instead, they sang many of their songs about gender dysphoria.

HB2, NORTH CAROLINA'S "BATHROOM BILL"

In March 2016, the State of North Carolina passed House Bill 2 (HB2), the Public Facilities Privacy & Security Act, which blocked cities statewide from allowing transgender individuals to use the bathroom consistent with their gender identity in public buildings and schools. The bill also prohibited cities from passing local nondiscrimination ordinances. It drew nationwide attention to North Carolina.

Several prominent musicians took a stand against the bill. Some, such as rock legend Bruce Springsteen, cancelled concerts they had planned in the state. Others, including Against Me! and Jimmy Buffet, chose to perform in the state as planned but used their concerts to speak out in protest of the bill.

In May 2016, US attorney general Loretta E. Lynch gave an empowering speech on the rights of the transgender community as she announced a US Department of Justice lawsuit against the state of North Carolina over HB2. Lynch addressed the transgender community directly, stating, "We see you; we stand with you; and we will do everything we can to protect you going forward."

Furthermore, Grace burned her birth certificate on stage as a powerful act of protest. As the paper burned, she spoke the words, "Goodbye, gender."

TRANSGENDER ROLE MODELS AND PIONEERS

Like punk rock, hip-hop has also carved out a space for queer and gender nonconforming artists. Alternative hip-hop star Mykki Blanco has expressed herself as multiple genders, identifying as transgender and gender fluid. She has used her music and art to promote inclusiveness and alternative gender expression. In 2015, Blanco also came out as HIV-positive and has used her platform to discuss HIV and other issues that face the LGBTQ community. Other hip-hop and R&B musicians, such as R&B singer Shamir, have identified as genderqueer or gender fluid. These artists represent a new era of greater acceptance of gender fluidity.

CHAPTER 4

TRANS WRITERS AND ARTISTS

The arts are another outlet humans use to express their opinions, share their experiences, and craft their own world. Several notable writers and artists who identify as transgender have contributed important work to highlight and share their life experiences.

JENNIFER FINNEY BOYLAN: THE FIRST TRANSGENDER BEST-SELLING AUTHOR

Jennifer Finney Boylan is a well-known transgender author and college professor. She graduated from Wesleyan University in 1980 and went to grad school for English at Johns Hopkins University. From 1988 to 2014, she was a professor at Colby College in Maine, after which she became a writer in residence at Barnard College at Columbia University, in New York City.

In 1988, Boylan married Deirdre Finney. The couple had two children together. In 2000, Boylan came out as transgender and began transitioning from male to female. She has spoken widely about how she believed her gender transition would cause her marriage to end. However, Finney stayed with Boylan through her transition and remained committed to their marriage.

In 2003, Boylan published *She's Not There: A Life in Two Genders*, an autobiography focused on her gender transition.

It became the first best seller written by a transgender author. During her book tour, Boylan and her wife talked openly about their marriage, family life, and the legal rights of the LGBTQ community. Boylan has written several memoirs and works of fiction. She has discussed her life and writing on various television shows—including *The Oprah Winfrey Show* and *Larry King Live*. In 2013, she became the first openly transgender cochair of GLAAD's National Board of Directors. That same year, she published *Stuck in the Middle with You: Parenthood in*

Succesful author and GLAAD board member Jennifer Finney Boylan appears at the 25th Annual GLAAD Media Awards in Los Angeles, California, on April 12, 2014.

Three Genders, in which she discussed her transition from the role of father to mother.

JANET MOCK: JOURNALIST AND BEST-SELLING AUTHOR

Born in Honolulu, Hawaii, in 1983, Janet Mock had three goals as a child: she wanted to be herself; she wanted to be a writer; and she wanted to live in New York City. As an adult, she would accomplish those goals, but not before a bumpy path to get there.

From a young age, Mock had identified as a woman. However, coming from a poor family, she could not afford the costs of a medical transition from male to female. At sixteen, she began engaging in prostitution to earn money for her transition. In January 2014, Mock published an essay on her website that acknowledged her past as a sex worker and drew attention to the fact that members of the transgender community often

Janet Mock has used her talents as a writer to pen essays and memoirs about her experiences as a transgender woman of color. Mock tackles difficult topics such as sex work and the high costs of transitioning.

must engage in sex work because of employment discrimination. In her essay, Mock writes:

> A leading factor that makes young trans women of color, like myself, more likely to engage in survival sex work is economic hardship. Family rejection and hostile, unwelcoming school environments can push a trans girl to leave these spaces, and anti-trans bias coupled with racism and misogyny and a lack of education heightens joblessness.

At first, Mock could afford female sex hormone pills only by getting them through a friend of hers at school. But she knew that what she was doing was dangerous, and so she came out as transgender to her mother. Concerned for her daughter's wellbeing, Mock's mother brought her to a doctor and helped her begin hormone-replacement therapy.

At the age of eighteen, Mock traveled to Thailand to undergo gender-affirmation surgery. The surgery was much cheaper there than it would have been in the United States. After returning, Mock completed college and moved to New York to pursue a master's in journalism at New York University. After graduating from NYU, Mock became a staff editor for *People* magazine.

In 2011, Mock came out as transgender in an essay for *Marie Clare*. The success of that essay made Mock a popular advocate. In 2012, she scored a book deal, and by 2014, she was able to publish her memoir *Redefining Realness: My Path to Womanhood, Identity, Love & So Much More*. The book, which tackled many of the complex issues faced by transgender women of color, debuted atop the *New York Times* Best Sellers List.

Mock's success as an author has allowed her to appear on numerous talk shows and in various publications advocating for transgender rights and helping provide appropriate language for discussing issues pertinent to the transgender community.

YOUNG & TRANS IN THE ARTS

Today, a new generation of transgender writers is creating more inclusive spaces for expressing the variety of transgender experiences. One notable example is Trace Peterson. Peterson is the author of the poetry collection *Since I Moved In (2007)* and coeditor of the anthology *Troubling the Line: Trans and Genderqueer Poetry and Poetics* (2013) along with TC Tolbert. In the fall of 2015, Peterson taught a course at Hunter College in New York City on transgender poetry. The course studied writings by twentieth- and twenty-first-century transgender and genderqueer poets.

In 2015, a group of young transgender poets collaborated for TRANS PLANET, a reading series that showcased their work and the work of other young transgender writers. Among the tour's readers were Jos Charles, founding editor of the transgender literary journal *Them*, and Manuel Arturo Abreu, who helped curate poets of color for the series.

The South Asian performing duo DarkMatter, which consists of Alok Vaid-Menon and Janani Balasubramanian, has performed at such prestigious venues as Lincoln Center and the Nuyorican Poets Cafe. DarkMatter's work challenges the very concept of gender

(continued on the next page)

(continued from the previous page)

Janani Blasubramanian and Alok Vaid-Menon of DarkMatter stand on stage at the La Mama Fall 2015 Gala in New York City. DarkMatter's work explores questions of gender, racism, and colonialism.

and explores the ways gender identity can be oppressive. Trans artist Juliana Huxtable has also received widespread attention for her work that includes elements of digital and African American culture. Her work has been featured at the New Museum as well as at the Museum of Modern Art.

LESLIE FEINBERG: BUTCH LESBIAN

Born in 1949 in Kansas City, Missouri, Leslie Feinberg was a writer and activist for the LGBTQ community. Her 1993 novel *Stone Butch Blues* explored the coming-of-age of a very butch lesbian teenager. (Butch lesbians are women who express their gender in a way traditionally associated with men.) The novel's main character considers transitioning from female to male, only to find herself alienated from the lesbian community. The novel highlights the reality that society's norms for gender expression do not always match a person's gender identity.

Feinberg represented the complexity of gender identity and expression in her own life. In a July 2006 interview with *Camp* magazine, Feinberg states, "I am female-bodied, I am a butch lesbian, a transgender lesbian." Feinberg used various gender pronouns depending on the context. Her 2006 novel *Drag King Dreams* addressed the lives of marginalized, working-class people in the transgender community and the violence transgender individuals face. Feinberg also wrote several nonfiction works on the history of the transgender rights movement. Most important among her nonfiction writings is *Transgender Warriors* (1996), which helped popularize gender studies and transgender terminology.

CHAPTER 5

TRANS ACTIVISTS

While transgender celebrities often become activists as a result of the platform their fame has given them, other members of the transgender community are known specifically for their activism. Activism is one of the most important tools for driving legal changes to better protect the rights of those who are transgender. The following are some of the most prominent trans activists who have worked to inspire policy changes.

STONEWALL RIOTS

Marsha P. Johnson and Sylvia Rivera were influential figures in New York City's LGBTQ scene starting in the 1960s. Johnson and Rivera both self-identified as drag queens. Johnson was African American, while Rivera was Latinx. Both activists were involved in the civil rights and feminism movements of the 1960s, but are most notable for their work in the gay liberation and transgender rights movement. Johnson participated in the June 1969 Stonewall Riots in New York City's Greenwich Village

Sylvia Rivera leads the activist group ACT-UP's march past New York City's Madison Square Park on June 26, 1994. The march commemorated the twenty-fifth anniversary of the 1969 Stonewall Riots.

neighborhood, during which members of the LGBTQ community clashed with local police.

Following the Stonewall Riots, Johnson and Rivera helped found various groups committed to gay and transgender activism. They were early members of the Gay Liberation Front and the Gay Activism Alliance, both of which formed in the immediate aftermath of the riots to seek greater political rights for members of the LGBTQ community. In 1970, the pair also formed Street Transvestite Action Revolutionaries (STAR), a group that worked to provide safe housing for transgender and genderqueer homeless youth. Rivera was also active in the Young Lords, a Puerto Rican nationalist group. In the 1980s, Johnson became an AIDS activist.

The work of Johnson and Rivera was crucial and is often understated. Both fought on multiple fronts for the civil rights of various minority groups, and they serve as a reminder of the important role of transgender and genderqueer figures in the early gay rights movement. Johnson was found dead in 1992. (Police ruled her death a suicide, but those close to her have always insisted she was murdered.) Rivera passed away in 2002 of liver cancer. The 2012 documentary *Pay It No Mind: The Life and Times of Marsha P. Johnson* documents the life of Johnson. In 2016, a Kickstarter-funded biopic of the lives of both activists, titled *Happy Birthday, Marsha!*, entered postproduction.

POLICY MAKERS

The important work of early transgender activists laid the groundwork for many of the legal protections that the LGBTQ community has secured today. Now, as transgender celebrities and activists increase awareness of discrimination against the transgender community and the need for greater legal protections, a new generation of activists is fighting for their community.

In 2015, Raffi Freedman-Gurspan became the first transgender person appointed to a staff position at the White House. A transgender woman of indigenous Central American origin, Freedman-Gurspan held several prominent roles prior to her appointment at the White House. Most notably, she was a policy advisor for the National Center for Transgender Equality. President Barack Obama first appointed Freedman-Gurspan to be an outreach and recruitment director in the Presidential Personnel Office. In 2016, she was also appointed as the White House's primary LGBTQ liaison.

Transgender activists are working on all fronts to promote the rights of the LGBTQ community. In March 2013, PFLAG,

Human rights activist Allyson Dylan Robinson *(left)* and PFLAG Director of Policy Diego Sanchez *(right)* appear at the 7th Annual PFLAG National Straight for Equality Awards Gala in New York City in March 2015.

an organization that supports family members and allies of LGBTQ people, appointed Diego Sanchez as its director of policy. Sanchez had formerly been a policy advisor for US Representative Barney Frank—an appointment that had made Sanchez the first openly transgender legislative staff member working in Washington, DC.

THE GLOBAL TRANS MOVEMENT

While detractors often—and incorrectly—argue that the transgender movement is a contemporary fad and a product of pop culture, there is a long documented history of transgender individuals in nearly all cultures. In South Asian cultures, there exists a third gender category known as *hijra* for transgender women. *Hijras* have achieved some degree of legal recognition and protection in Pakistan, Bangladesh, and India. In many Native American cultures, there exist two-spirit people, gender nonconforming individuals who traditionally have performed special spiritual roles in their communities.

TRANS TEEN ACTIVISTS

An emerging generation of transgender activists is forming, and these pioneers are starting younger than any of their predecessors. Jazz Jennings is known for having been one of the youngest people yet to document her gender dysphoria and transition publicly. She was only four when doctors diagnosed her gender dysphoria. By the time she was six, Jazz and her supportive family were appearing on talk shows, including *20/20*, to promote awareness about the challenges faced by transgender youth. A 2011 documentary, *I Am Jazz: A Family in Transition*, shared Jazz's story. It was later followed by a reality show, *I Am Jazz*, in 2015.

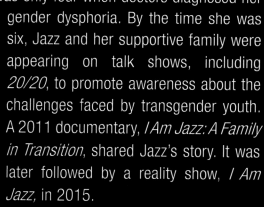

Nicole Maines, a transgender student from Maine, fought from the time she was in fifth grade for her right to use the girls' bathroom at school. In 2014, when she was sixteen, the Supreme Court of Maine upheld her right to use women's facilities. Nicole, who has a cisgender twin brother,

At a young age, Jazz Jennings became a spokesperson for transgender children, highlighting their struggles and need for

had her story told in the 2015 biography *Becoming Nicole: The Transformation of an American Family.*

In 2015, Lila Perry, a seventeen-year-old transgender student in Missouri, made the news after using the girls' locker room at school. A group of students at her school protested and organized a walkout, demanding that Lila use the boys' locker room. Lila and her supporters organized a support rally in response. Lila told reporters,

> **I believe that there are places like Hillsboro all over the county where young people are hurting, feeling alone, and being discriminated against because of who they are. And I believe it's important, now that I've been put in this position, for me to stay strong for all of those young people and for my community.**

Beyond the United States, there is a global trans movement to protect the rights of the transgender community everywhere. In 2012, Argentina became the first nation to pass a gender identity law, allowing the country's transgender community to legally register as such and obtain identity documents (and, therefore, work). The law was the result of more than a decade's worth of advocacy by Lohana Berkins, founder of the Asociación de Lucha por la Identidad Travesti y Transexual (Association for the Struggle for Travesti and Transsexual Identity). In 2013, Bindiya Rana fought for and won her right to run for election in a provincial assembly as Pakistan's first transgender candidate. In India, Lakshmi Narayan Tripathi's long campaign for the rights of the *hijra* community helped lead to a 2014 Supreme Court decision formally recognizing the rights of India's *hijra* community as a legal third gender.

Members of the Association of Transgender/Hijra in Bengal (ATHB) hold up a banner as they celebrate Transgender Day 2016 outside the Academy of Fine Arts in Kolkata, India.

Activists in the trans community of all ages, backgrounds, and nationalities have fought for greater recognition and legal protections. These role models will long be remembered as the pioneers who helped create a safe, dignified, and more inclusive community for transgender and gender nonconforming individuals everywhere.

GLOSSARY

ADVOCATE A person who works publicly to advance or promote a certain cause.

ALLURE A charming or attractive quality or power.

ANDROGYNOUS Neither discernibly male nor female in qualities or characteristics.

CHARADE A deceptive act performed to convince others.

CISGENDER Having a gender identity that matches the one a person was assigned at birth.

DETRIMENTAL Harmful or having a negative effect.

DYSTOPIAN Related to an imaginary or fictional place where everyone is unhappy and treated poorly.

GENDER-AFFIRMATION SURGERY Any doctor-supervised surgical intervention that a transgender person may choose to undergo in order to better express their gender.

GENDER DYSPHORIA The distress or depression produced by an incongruity between one's gender identity (the gender that a person internally feels that they are) and the gender one has been assigned.

GENDER FLUID Having a gender identity or gender expression that is not fixed and may change between male or female multiple times.

GENDERQUEER Having a gender expression is neither strictly male nor female, but rather blends elements of gender expression traditionally associated with both genders.

LATINX A gender-inclusive form of the word "Latino," often used by Latinos who are genderqueer.

TRANSGENDER ROLE MODELS AND PIONEERS

LGBTQ Acronym for "lesbian, gay, bisexual, transgender, and queer/questioning."

LUCRATIVE Well paying or very profitable.

OPHTHALMOLOGIST A doctor who specializes in surgical and medical issues related to the eye.

OUT To reveal that somebody identifies as LGBTQ.

TRANSGENDER A person whose gender identity does not match the one they were assigned at birth.

UNPRECEDENTED Never seen or experienced before.

FOR MORE INFORMATION

Canadian Professional Association for Transgender Health (CPATH)
201-1770 Fort Street
Victoria, BC V8R 1J5
Canada
(250) 592-6183
Website: http://www.cpath.ca
CPATH is the largest national multidisciplinary, professional
organization in the world working to support the health,
well-being, and dignity of trans and gender-diverse people.

GLAAD
5455 Wilshire Boulevard, #1500
Los Angeles, CA 90036
(323) 933-2240
Website: http://www.glaad.org
GLAAD works to amplify the voice of the LGBT community.
The organization works for cultural change and "promotes
understanding, increases acceptance, and advances
equality."

National Center for Transgender Equality (NCTE)
1400 16th Street NW, Suite 510
Washington, DC 20036
(202) 642-4542
Website: http://www.transequality.org
The National Center for Transgender Equality (NCTE) is the
country's leading social justice advocacy organization for
transgender people. Founded in 2003, NCTE advocates for

transgender issues at the local, state, and federal levels, working to change laws, policies, and societal attitudes.

PFLAG Canada
331 Cooper Street, Suite 200
Ottawa, ON K2P 0G5
Canada
(888) 530-6777
Website: https://www.pflagcanada.ca/en/index.html
PFLAG Canada is Canada's only national organization that helps all Canadians with issues of sexual orientation, gender identity, and gender expression. PFLAG Canada provides support, education, and resources.

Transgender Law Center
1629 Telegraph Avenue, Suite 400
Oakland, CA 94612
(415) 865-0176
Website: http://transgenderlawcenter.org
Transgender Law Center works to change laws, policies, and attitudes so that all people can live safely, authentically, and free from discrimination regardless of their gender identity or expression.

Trans Lifeline
San Francisco, CA
United States: (877) 565-8860
Canada: (877) 330-6366
Website: http://hotline.translifeline.org
Trans Lifeline offers a hotline that is "staffed by transgender people for transgender people." Its culturally competent service is free

and confidential, empowering those going through the "darkest moments of their lives," namely gender-identity struggles and suicide.

Trans Youth Equality Foundation
PO Box 7441
Portland, ME 04112
(207) 478-4087
Website: http://www.transyouthequality.org
The Trans Youth Equality Foundation offers support, advocacy, and education for transgender and gender nonconforming youth and their families.

TransYouth Family Allies
PO Box 1471
Holland, MI 49422
(888) 462-8932
Website: http://www.imatyfa.org
This nonprofit organization teams up with educators, service providers, and communities to foster supportive environments in which gender can be expressed and respected without violence and suicide.

WEBSITES

Because of the changing nature of internet links, Rosen Publishing has developed an online list of websites related to the subject of this book. This site is updated regularly. Please use this link to access the list:

http://www.rosenlinks.com/TL/role

FOR FURTHER READING

Andrews, Arin. *Some Assembly Required: The Not-So-Secret Life of a Transgender Teen.* New York, NY: Simon and Schuster Books for Young Readers, 2014.

Bono, Chaz, and Billie Fitzpatrick. *Transition: Becoming Who I Was Always Meant to Be.* New York, NY: Penguin, 2011.

Grinapol, Corinne. *Harvey Milk: Pioneering Gay Politician.* New York, NY: Rosen Publishing, 2015.

Herthel, Jessica, and Jazz Jennings. *I Am Jazz.* New York, NY: Dial Books, 2014.

Hill, Katie Rain. *Rethinking Normal: A Memoir in Transition.* New York, NY: Simon and Schuster Books for Young Readers, 2014.

Kuklin, Susan. *Beyond Magenta: Transgender Teens Speak Out.* Somerville, MA: Candlewick, 2015.

Mapua, Jeff. *Lana Wachowski.* New York, NY: Rosen Publishing, 2016.

Mock, Janet. *Redefining Realness: My Path to Womanhood, Identity, Love & So Much More.* New York, NY: Atria Books, 2014.

Mooney, Carla. *Caitlyn Jenner.* New York, NY: Rosen Publishing, 2016.

Nagle, Jeanne. *GLBT Teens and Society.* New York, NY: Rosen Publishing, 2010.

Shultz, Jackson Wright. *Trans/Portraits: Voices from Transgender Communities.* Lebanon, NH: Dartmouth College Press, 2015.

Staley, Erin. *Laverne Cox.* New York, NY: Rosen Publishing, 2016.

Tesla, Rylan Jay, et al. *The Gender Quest Workbook: A Guide for Teens and Young Adults Exploring Gender Identity.* Oakland, CA: Instant Help, 2015.

BIBLIOGRAPHY

Bakkila, Blake. "The Transgender Heroines Who Started a Revolution: Video Series Explores Activists' Hidden History—and a Possible Murder." *People*, March 1, 2016. http://www.people.com/people/article/weve-been-around-transgender-docuseries-marsha-johnson-sylvia-rivera.

Bissinger, Buzz. "Caitlyn Jenner: The Full Story." *Vanity Fair*, July 2015.http://www.vanityfair.com/hollywood/2015/06/caitlyn-jenner-bruce-cover-annie-leibovitz.

Boylan, Jennifer Finney. "Is My Marriage Gay?" *New York Times*, May 11, 2009. http://www.nytimes.com/2009/05/12/opinion/12boylan.html?_r=1&.

Brady, Erik. "Transgender Male Kye Allums on the Women's Team at GW." *USA Today*, November 3, 2010. http://usatoday30.usatoday.com/sports/college/womensbasketball/atlantic10/2010-11-03-kye-allums-george-washington-transgender_N.htm.

Breen, Matthew. "Laverne Cox: The Making of an Icon." *Advocate*, July 10, 2014. http://www.advocate.com/print-issue/current-issue/2014/07/10/laverne-cox-making-icon.

Chapman, Alex. "The Multiplicities of Mykki Blanco." *Interview*, April 4, 2012. http://www.interviewmagazine.com/culture/mykki-blanco/#_.

Grinberg, Emanuella. "Bathroom Access for Transgender Teen Divides Missouri Town." CNN, September 5, 2015. http://www.cnn.com/2015/09/03/living/missouri-transgender-teen-feat.

Hadjimatheou, Chloe. "Christine Jorgensen: 60 Years of Sex Change Ops." BBC News, November 30, 2012. http://www

.bbc.com/news/magazine-20544095.

Hainey, Michael. "The Woman Who Paved the Way for Men to Become Women." *GQ*, May 26, 2015. http://www.gq.com/story/renee-richards-interview.

Hemon, Aleksander. "Beyond the Matrix." *New Yorker*, September 10, 2012. http://www.newyorker.com/magazine/2012/09/10/beyond-the-matrix.

Herman, Robin. "'No Exceptions,' and No Renee Richards." *New York Times*, August 27, 1976. https://www.nytimes.com/packages/html/sports/year_in_sports/08.27.html.

Jeltsen, Melissa. "Why This Transgender Teen's Big Victory Matters." Huffington Post, February 3, 2014. http://www.huffingtonpost.com/2014/02/03/transgender-rights_n_4705613.html.

Kopan, Tal, and Eugene Scott. "North Carolina Governor Signs Controversial Transgender Bill." CNN Politics, March 24, 2016. http://www.cnn.com/2016/03/23/politics/north-carolina-gender-bathrooms-bill.

Lambe, Stacy. "An Oral History of Transgender Representation on Scripted TV." *Out*, December 16, 2015. http://www.out.com/television/2015/12/16/transgender-representation-scripted-tv-oral-history.

Lamphier, Jason. "Artists of DarkMatter: 'Let's Challenge the Standards of Trans Visibility.'" *Out*, May 17, 2016. www.out.com/hit-list/2016/5/17/artists-darkmatter-lets-challenge-standards-trans-visibility.

MacDonald-Dupuis, Natasha. "Meet Wendy Carlos: The Trans Godmother of Electronic Music." *Thump*, August 11, 2015. https://thump.vice.com/en_us/article/meet-wendy-carlos-the-trans-godmother-of-electronic-music.

Mock, Janet, and Kierna Mayo. "I Was Born a Boy." *Marie Clare*,

May 18, 2011. http://www.marieclaire.com/sex-love/advice/a6075/born-male.

Reed, Susan. "After a Sex Change and Several Eclipses, Wendy Carlos Treads a New Digital Moonscape." *People*, July 1, 1985. http://www.people.com/people/archive/article/0,,20091206,00.html.

Rolling Stone. "Tom Gabel of Against Me! Comes Out as Transgender." May 8, 2012. http://www.rollingstone.com/music/news/tom-gabel-of-against-me-comes-out-as-transgender-20120508.

Saether, Logan. "NewHive hosts an intriguing first Trans Planet Online Reading." *State Press*, October 26, 2015. http://www.statepress.com/article/2015/10/new-hive-trans-planet-reading.

Segal, Corinne. "Poet Creates First Class for Transgender Poetry." PBS Newshour, July 27, 2015. http://www.pbs.org/newshour/poetry/poet-moves-create-first-class-transgender-poetry.

Steinmetz, Katy. "Laverne Cox Talks to *TIME* About the Transgender Movement." *Time*, May 29, 2014. http://time.com/132769/transgender-orange-is-the-new-black-laverne-cox-interview.

Sylvia Rivera Law Project. "Who Was Sylvia Rivera?" Retrieved June 15, 2016. http://srlp.org/about/who-was-sylvia-rivera.

Weber, Bruce. "Leslie Feinberg, Writer and Transgender Activist, Dies at 65." *New York Times*, November 24, 2014. http://www.nytimes.com/2014/11/25/nyregion/leslie-feinberg-writer-and-transgender-activist-dies-at-65.html?_r=0.

Webber, Stephanie. "Lilly Wachowski Makes First Public Appearance Since Coming Out as Transgender." *Us Weekly*, April 3, 2016. http://www.usmagazine.com/celebrity-news/news/-w201210.

1NDEX